My Christmas Journal & Activity Book

Deirdre Shahzad

Independently Published on Amazon by CKB Press

13 Shannon Cove, Dromod,
Co. Leitrim, Republic of Ireland
Email: info@ckbpress.com
Website: www.ckbpress.com

First Edition

ISBN: 978-1-914133-08-4

Dedication

To my lovely children.

Contents

About me

Having spent over 15 years in the travel industry and now a mom of 3, 2 of whom have additional needs, I could see how there was a huge number of special needs parents who were so consumed by fear of the unknown they could not bring themselves to even think of a day out, let alone a holiday with their children.

There were lots of opinions of what you should have, or 'I think' you can have floating around. Opinions on what is good and what is not and more often than not I, would look on in horror at the 'advice' that would be given.

A lot of the time it would be either incorrect or just not suitable for the child in questions needs.

This drove me to create www.autismandadventures.com.

A place, where I could combine both my knowledge and love of the travel industry with my knowledge of what the needs are of parents out there to ensure a fun family holiday and respite for the entire family.

A place, where you, as a parent, could ensure the information you were receiving was clear and correct.

This in turn drove me to create my first book My Travel and Activity Journal.

Created, with the idea in mind, of allowing the child to participate throughout the whole process: to visualise themselves there and to sign post their entire journey, while also paving the way for future trips.

I wanted to create something that they could not only entertain and occupy their minds while travelling but hopefully ease any anxieties they may have of the unknown in a fun way.

Once this book was completed, I realised that the same principal could be applied to many other aspects of our children's lives. Christmas being a big one.

With so many areas for sensory overload, Christmas can be a real source of stress for parents and children alike.

This journal breaks down each event of a child's Christmas in the hopes it can become more manageable for them to digest and ultimately enjoy...

4

How to use this book

The about me section is a quick guide on your child that they could show anyone whether staff, teachers or family member visiting.

The entire journal has been created in a way that your child can look positively at their experiences and almost like a scrapbook and keepsake to revert upon.

Knowing, the anxieties that Christmas can have on a child on the spectrum, I felt it important to breakdown each area bit by bit in more manageable bite size chunks for them to digest.

Christmas can be such a busy time for everyone, we can sometimes forget how much our kids can feel overwhelmed with it all.

Even something that would appear on the surface as insignificant to us, can be a huge trigger for our kids.

There are lots of colouring pages and puzzles to keep your child occupied throughout the Christmas holiday season, with something to suit all, including some craft and baking sections.

Art and baking are great calming sensory activities for when things can get too much.

I have purposely created, the book in black and white to avoid any issues around certain colours or colour combinations.

This also leaves the journal open to be fully personalised by your child.

I hope both you and your child enjoy completing the activities and have a truly memorable and fantastic Christmas.

Merry Christmas

Deirdre x

Christmas

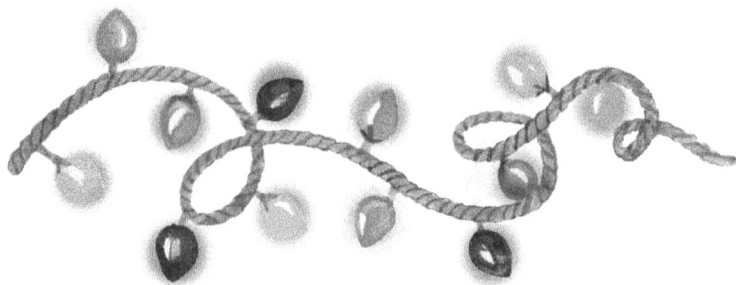

Christmas is a lovely time of year filled with lots of magic and sparkle.

We celebrate the birth of Jesus by decorating our houses with brightly decorated trees and tinsel.

We meet with friends and family, exchange presents and if we have been very good, we may even get a visit from Santa Claus on Christmas Eve.

In this book we are going to explore the magic of Christmas and have lots of fun along the way.

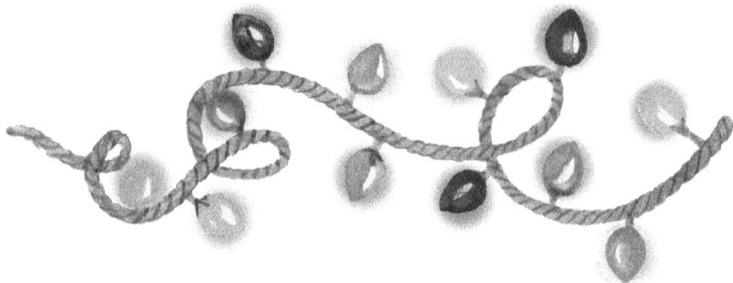

This book belongs to

I am _____ years old

I live with my _____

_____

This is a picture of our family.

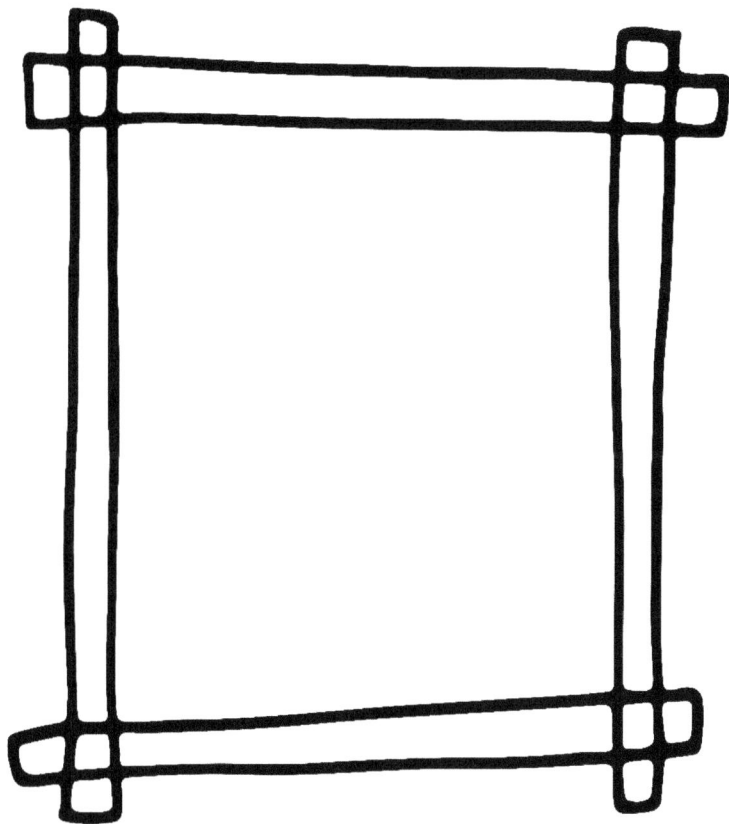

9

My favourite part of Christmas time is:

When I think of Christmas, I feel

Sometimes Christmas time can make people feel strange. They can get a funny feeling in their tummy or they might not like all the loud music or bright lights, and this is ok.

It's Ok to feel nervous or scared just as much as its ok to enjoy everything and have lots of fun.

When you think of Christmas now, how do you feel?

Draw a picture of the things, if any, that worry you around Christmas time.

Countdown to Christmas

Today is

That means we have _____

sleeps until Christmas Eve.

Countdown the steps

1	2	3	4	5
6	7	8	9	10
11	12	13	14	15
16	17	18	19	20
21	2	22	24	Christmas

Christmas Traditions

There are lots of traditions at Christmas.

A tradition is something that we do to celebrate an occasion every time it happens, like having a cake on your birthday.

HOLLY
& JOLLY

Draw or write some of your family traditions at Christmas.

_____

_____

_____

_____

_____

_____

_____

_____

_____

_____

_____

_____

_____

Our family traditions

18

Your Christmas Tree

One of the biggest traditions at Christmas is putting up the decorations.

We will decorate our Christmas tree with lots of lights and baubles. We might even put some tinsel on the tree.

We put either a:

Star ☐

Fairy ☐

On top of our tree.

Draw a picture of your decorated Christmas tree

My Christmas Tree

Imagine you could make your own Christmas bauble. What would it look like? Use the space below to draw it....

My Christmas Bauble

Christmas Shopping

Today we are going Christmas shopping.

We will visit _____

I will leave home at _____

Our shopping list:

_____

_____

_____

_____

_____

_____

_____

Sometimes, shops can be loud and noisy.

If I get scared or anxious, I have 5 ways to help me.

They are:

1. Tell an adult I am upset

2. Play with my favourite toy

3. Wear my ear defenders

4. Watch my device

5. Play a game like counting how many red coats there are.

Draw a picture of you at the shops

Draw a picture of something you will buy.

What did you enjoy on your shopping trip?

_____

_____

What did you not like about your shopping trip?

_____

_____

What could you do differently next time?

_____

_____

_____

Visiting Santa

We are going to visit Santa at:

_____

When we get there, we will wait our turn to see him.

There will be other boys and girls waiting to see him too.

We will all be very excited.

When I meet Santa, I can sit on his lap, or the floor, or with my family.

Draw a picture of you visiting Santa.

Santa and me

HOLLY
& JOLLY

MERRY
& BRIGHT

I will tell Santa what I would like to receive on Christmas Eve.

I can tell him using my words or by drawing him a picture.

I can also send Santa a letter.

On the next page is a letter you can get an adult to cut out and post, to give to Santa on your visit.

MERRY

CHRISTMAS

My Wish List

Dear Santa

My name is

_____

I am _____ years old.

I have been   very good ☐

                           extra good ☐

                    super duper good ☐

This year I would like:

SANTA KLAUS * HO! HO! HO!
25 12
APPROVED LETTER

_____
_____
_____
_____
_____
_____
_____
_____
_____

Write about your time with Santa.

What did you enjoy?

_____

_____

What did you not like?

_____

_____

What could we do differently?

_____

_____

_____

_____

PASSED
DE / 25

Your School Play

At Christmas time our school have a play for all the parents to come and watch.

We dress up in costumes, learn some lovely songs to sing together and some children even have lines they say out loud.'

This year our class play is about

_____

I will be _____

in the play.

When we are finished the parents will clap and cheer.

38

Draw a picture of you in your play.

My School Play

Think about your school play.

What did you enjoy?

_____

_____

What did you not like?

_____

_____

What could you do differently?

_____

_____

_____

Draw a picture or add a photo to the frame.

Christmas Eve

Today is Christmas Eve.

We will do:

_____

_____

_____

_____

I must go to sleep on time tonight so Santa can come and leave a present under our tree.

At bedtime, I will have a bath /shower, get into my PJs and leave some treats for Santa and the reindeer.

What treats will you leave out?

Treats for Santa and the reindeer

Draw a picture or add a photo to the frame.

Christmas Day

Merry Christmas!

It's Christmas morning!!!

Santa came and left some lovely gifts.

Draw a picture of your favourite gift.

My favourite gift

Today is a special day.

On Christmas Day, some people go to church, visit family, have family visit them, or have a lovely dinner together.

What will your family do today?

Christmas Day

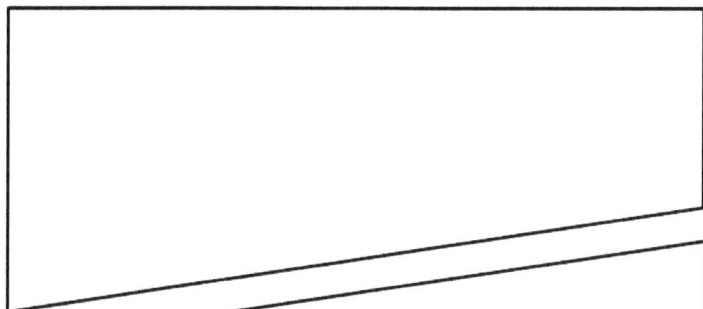

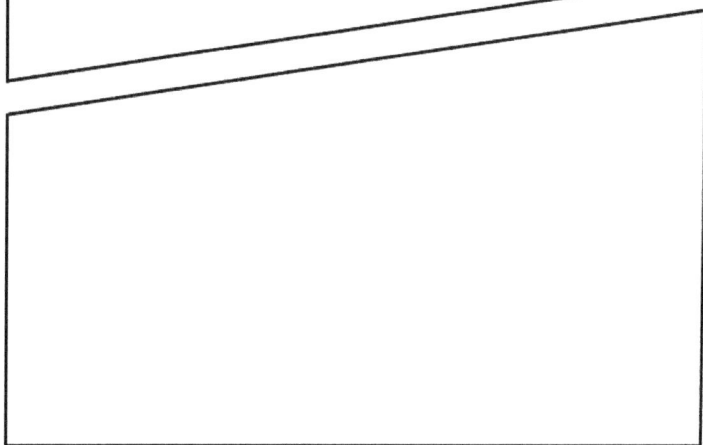

51

Draw a picture or add a photo to the frame.

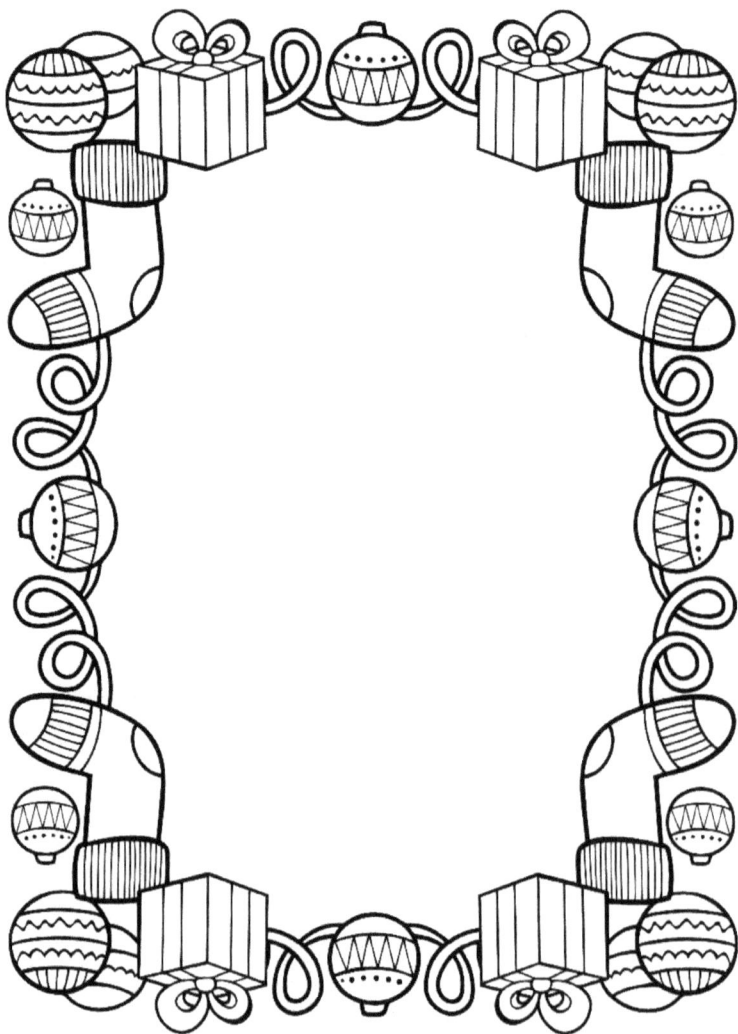

After Christmas

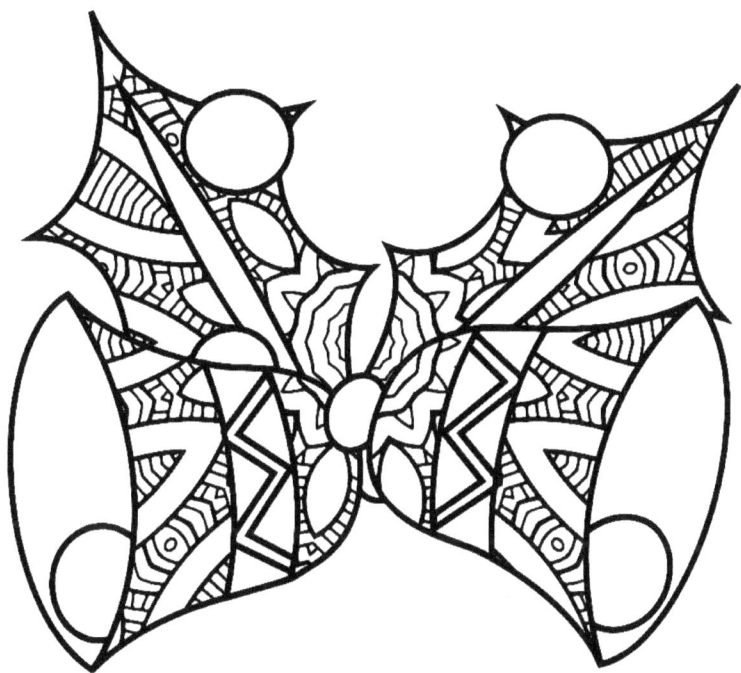

When Christmas is over, we will take down all our decorations and pack them away until next year.

We had lots of fun this year and did lots of cool things.

Draw a picture of some of your favourite things from this year.

My favourite things over Christmas:

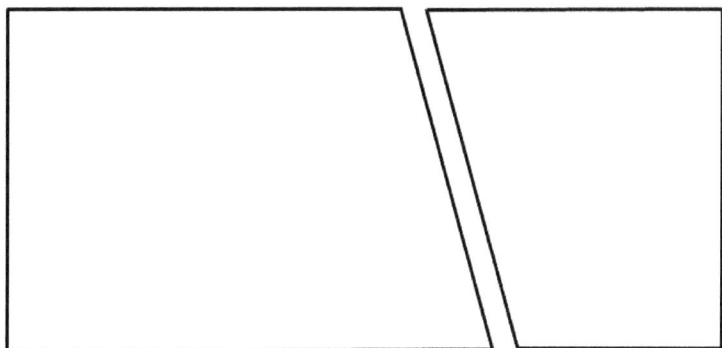

Draw a picture or add a photo to the frame.

Recipes

57

Strawberry Santa's

You'll need:

- Some strawberries
- Double cream that has been whisked. You could also use crème fraise.

Cut the stalks off the strawberries, leaving a flat edge.

Cut the point from the strawberry about 1/3 down.

Place a spoonful of cream on the larger half of the strawberry and put strawberry point on top to make a Santa hat.

Add a pinch of cream at the point.

You can also add eyes, buttons and feet if you'd like...

Sugar Cookies

Ingredients:

- 375g plain flour
- 1 tsp baking powder
- ½ tsp salt
- 225 g butter softened
- 200g caster sugar
- 1 large egg
- 1 tsp vanilla essence
- 1 tbsp milk

Instructions:

In a bowl, mix together the flour, baking powder and salt. Set aside.

In another bowl, beat the butter and sugar until fluffy and pale.

Add the egg, milk and vanilla and beat until combined.

Gradually add the flour until fully combined.

Shape into a ball, wrap with some cling film and chill in the fridge for 1 hour.

After 1 hour

Pre-heat the over to 180 °C/gas 6

Line 2 baking sheets with parchment.

Take your mix out of the fridge.

Lightly flour your surface so that the mixture doesn't stick to it.

Using a rolling pin, roll your dough out until it's 1/8th in or ¼ cm thick.

Cut into shapes and place on your baking trays.

Tip: So your shapes will hold, freeze for approximately 10 mins.

Bake until the edges start to turn golden (around 8 - 10 minutes)

Decorate with icing or fondant.

Gingerbread Men

Ingredients:

175g dark muscovado sugar

85g golden syrup

100 butter

350g plain flour

1 tsp bicarbonate of soda

1 tbsp ground ginger

1 tsp ground cinnamon

1 egg beaten

Instructions:

Melt the butter sugar and golden syrup in a pan.

Once bubbling for 1-2 minutes, take of the stove and leave to cool.

In a bowl, put the spices, bicarbonate of soda, and flour and mix.

Next add the sugar mixture and the egg.

Stir all together.

Knead in the bowl until smooth.

Wrap in cling wrap and chill for at least 30 minutes.

When ready remove from fridge and leave until room temperature and softened.

Preheat your oven 220ºC/180ºC/gas 6.

Line 2 baking trays with parchment.

Roll out your dough until its around 2mm thick.

Use a cutter and cut out your men.

Bake for 10-12 mins, checking halfway.

Leave to cool on a tray then cool on a rack completely.

Decorate with icing, sweets or melted chocolate.

They will keep for up to 3 days when kept in a sealed container.

Cupcakes

Ingredients:

250g Self raising Flour (all purpose)

250g Caster Sugar

250g Butter/baking margarine

4 eggs

50ml milk

Buttercream to decorate

Instructions:

In a bowl, beat the butter until soft,

Add the sugar and beat until fluffy.

Next beat in the eggs one at a time.

Add the sifted flour and milk, mix until all combined.

Divide the mixture into a cupcake tin lined with paper cases. Bake in a preheated oven at 150 for 25 mins.

As an optional extra you could add a few drops of

vanilla extract or paste with the flour.

Once baked remove from the oven and allow to cool completely before decorating with for example buttercream icing.

Buttercream Icing

Ingredients:

250g Real dairy Butter at room temperature

500g Icing sugar

50ml milk or boiling water

Instructions:

Place you butter in a mixing bowl and beat for at least 5 mins on a high speed.

Gradually add your sifted icing sugar until it is all combined.

Add your milk or water to create a smooth silky buttercream and beat to combine.

If you would like to colour your buttercream decide how many colours you would like.

If more than one colour, then divide the mixture equally and add a few drops of gel colour and mix through.

Now you can decorate your cooled cupcakes using your choice of piping bag and nozzle or spoon onto the top of the bun and add any other decorations you wish.

Draw a picture or add a photo to the frame.

Crafts

Pinecone Christmas Tree

Collect some pinecones on your next walk in the forest or park.

Paint them green.

When they are fully dry, add some coloured dots with either paint, sequins or pompoms.

Hand print wreath

You will need:

- Paper plate
- Pencil or marker
- Green paper or white paper with green paint
- Ribbon/ String
- Safety scissors
- PVA glue or pritt stick

Method:

If using the green paper place your hand down and draw around it. Alternatively, paint your hand with green paint and make prints onto the white paper. You will need at least 20 handprints depending on the size of your hand.

Once dried cut out all the hands.

Take your paper plate and cut out the central circle, leaving just a ring.

Glue each hand print onto the paper plate ring giving you a wreath, making sure you cant see any of the paper plate.

You can design your wreat as you wish using pom pom's, sequins or glitter.

Once the glue is dry on the hand prints turn your wreath around and glue the ribbon onto the back so you can hang it up.

You can use any colour combination that you wish for the handprints. If you have brothers and sisters why not use both your hand prints and each use a different colour.

Salt dough ornaments

Salt Dough Ornaments

You will need:
- 2 cups of plain flour
- 1 cup table salt
- 1 cup warm water
- Cutters
- Rolling pin
- Skewer
- Twine or ribbon

Method:

Preheat the oven to its lowest setting and line a baking sheet with baking parchment.
Mix the flour and salt in a large bowl. Add the water and stir until it comes together into a ball.
Transfer the dough to a floured work surface, your dough should be smooth and silky. If its a bit sticky add a little bit more flour.

Once you've kneaded your dough for a few mins, roll out until its about ¼ inch thick. Now you can cut it into any shapes you like. Not forgetting to cut a little hole at the top with your skewer.
Put your finished items on the lined baking sheet and bake for 3 hrs or until solid.
Leave to cool and then paint and decorate as you wish.
Once decorated thread your twine or ribbon through the hole made prior to baking

Snow Globe

You will need:
- Small glass jar with lid
- A plastic figurine or small decoration
- Glycerin
- Glitter
- Sequins
- Water
- Spoon
- Superglue or a hot glue gun

Method:

Choose some small toys or Christmas figures and arrange them onto the inside of the jar lid. Once you are happy with how they look glue them into place.
Fill the jar water leaving a gap at the top to allow for the figures.
Place 2-3 teaspoons of glitter and or sequins and mix with a spoon.
Add a few drops of glycerine into the jar this will help the glitter float.

Once the glue is dry on the lid, screw the lid onto the jar and turn upside down and shake and enjoy.

*If you feel you haven't added enough water top it up now, if you are happy with the water level run a line of glue on the inside of the lid and screw back into place to ensure it can't be unscrewed again.

Draw a picture or add a photo to the frame.

Colouring Pages

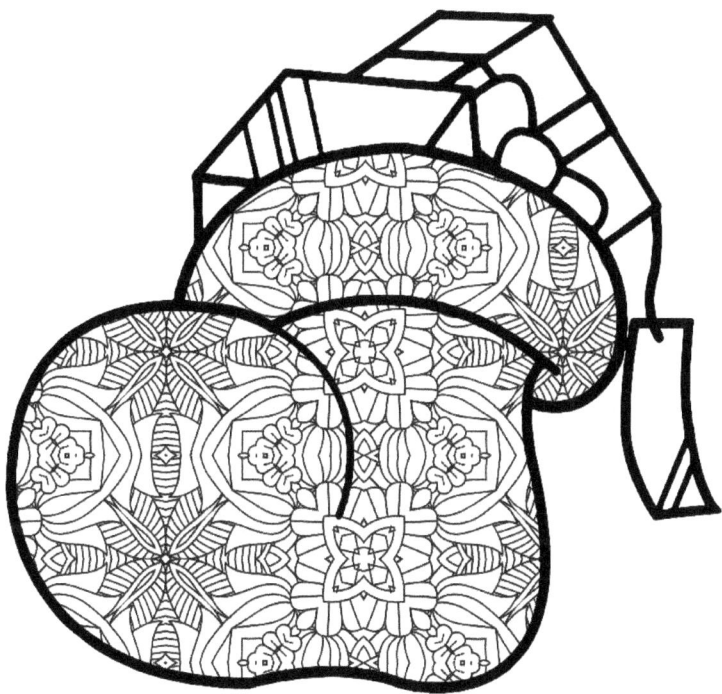

fun Activities

What comes next?

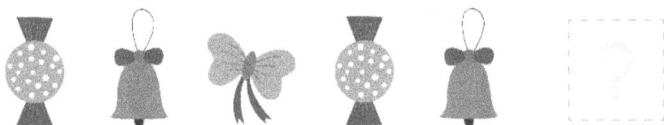

Whose gingerbread?

91

Join the dots

Follow the numbers in order to create the picture

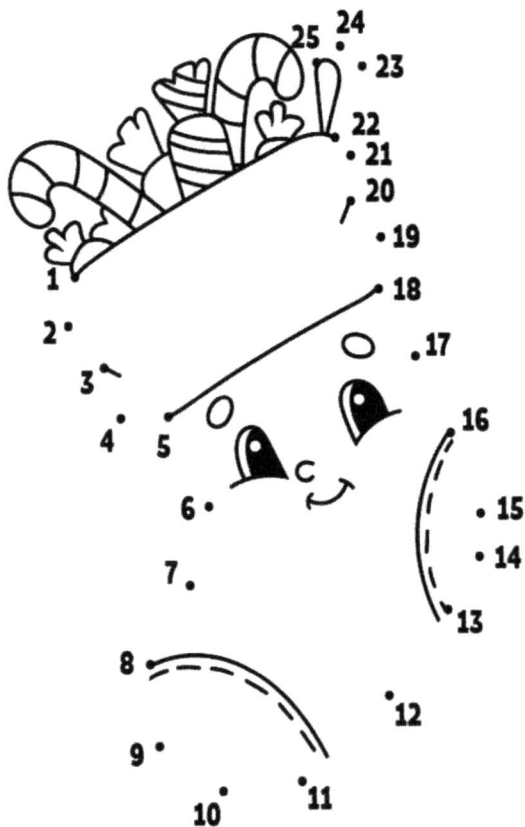

Join the dots

Follow the numbers in order to create the picture

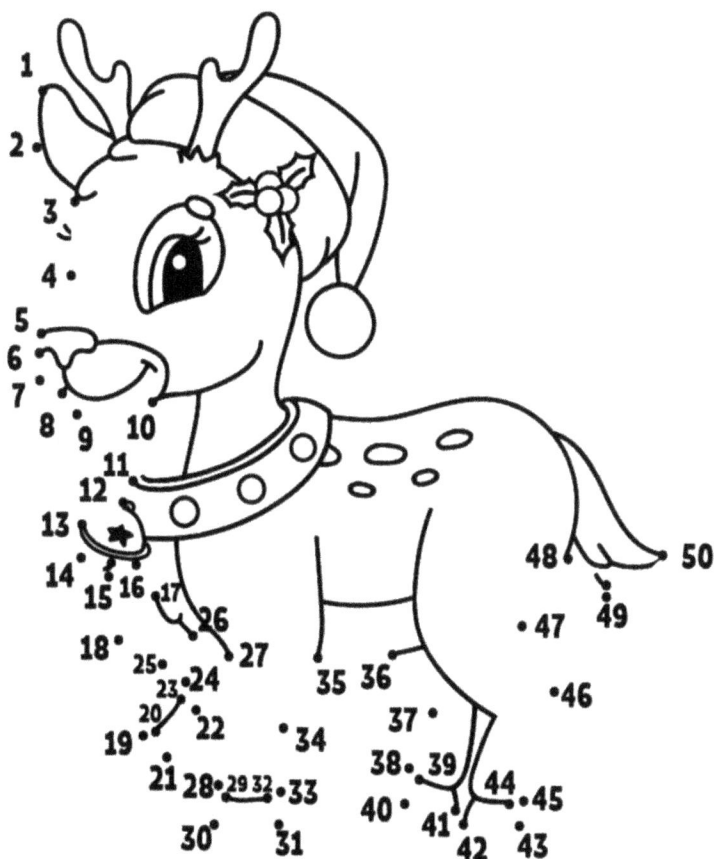

Join the dots

Follow the numbers in order to create the picture

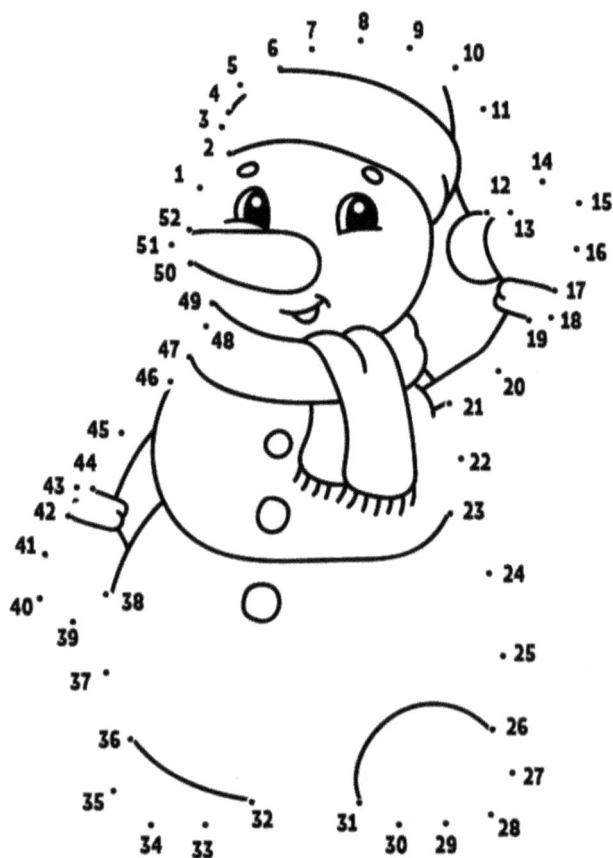

Join the dots

Follow the numbers in order to create the picture

Join the dots

Follow the numbers in order to create the picture

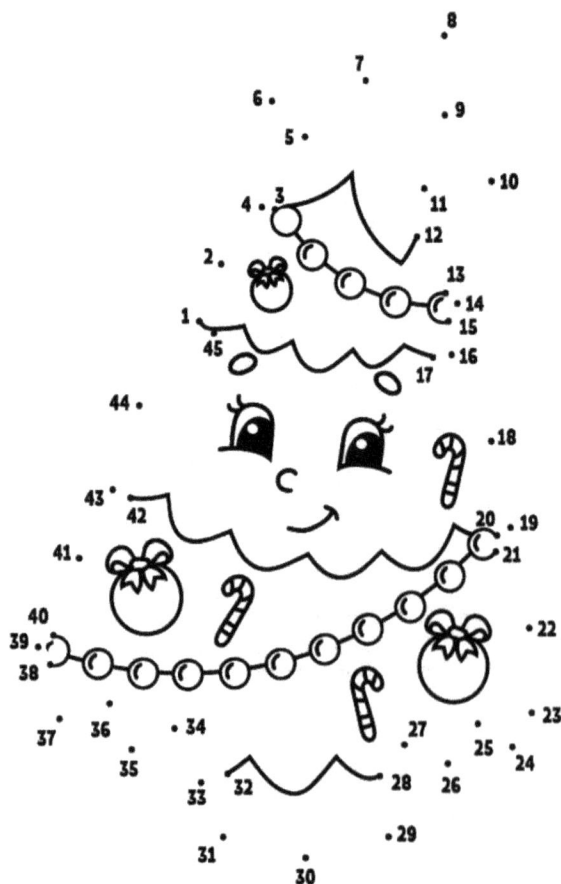

Puzzles and Games

Tic Tac Toe instructions

Tic-tac-toe (also known as noughts and crosses) is an easy and fun game in which two players take turns to see who can get three in a row first.

The first person wins the game.

The game is played on a grid of 9 boxes.

X's and O's are used as the markers

X	**O**	
X	**X**	**O**
O		**X**

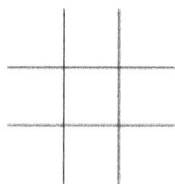 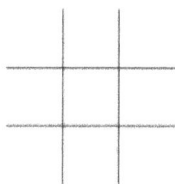 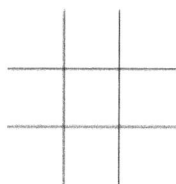

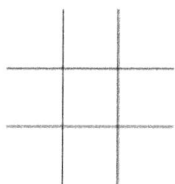 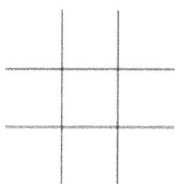 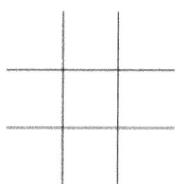

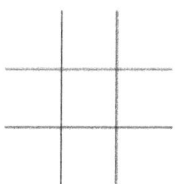 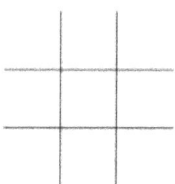 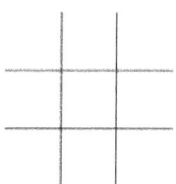

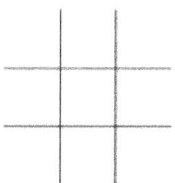 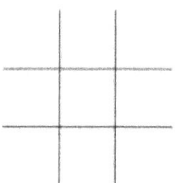 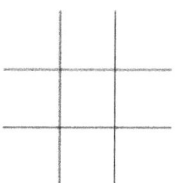

Tic Tac Toe - 2

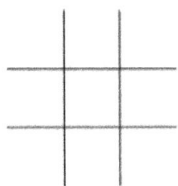 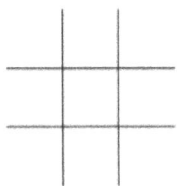 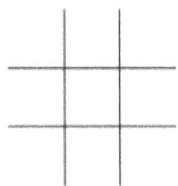

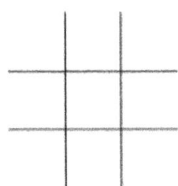 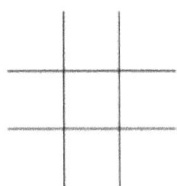 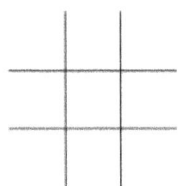

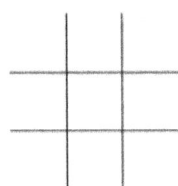 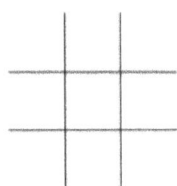 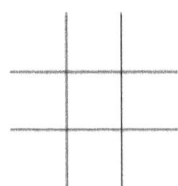

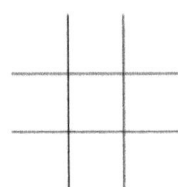 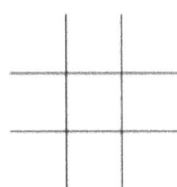 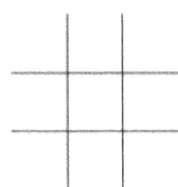

Tic Tac Toe - 3

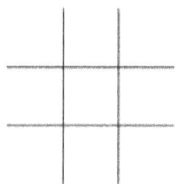 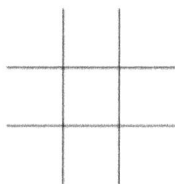 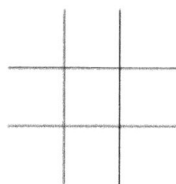

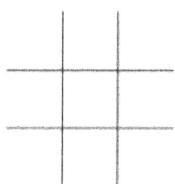 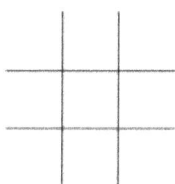 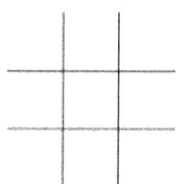

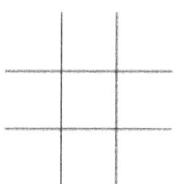 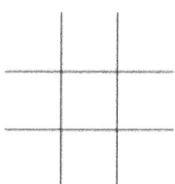 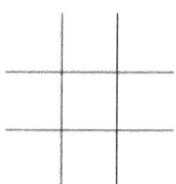

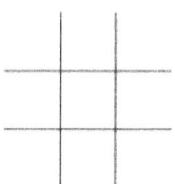 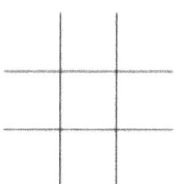 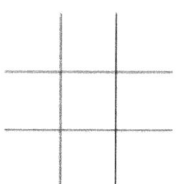

Tic Tac Toe - 4

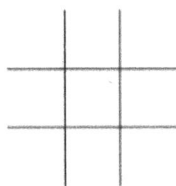 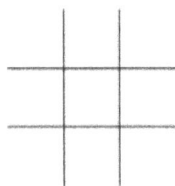 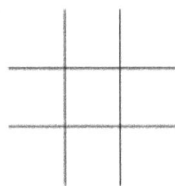

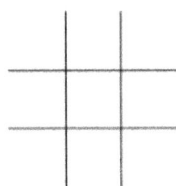 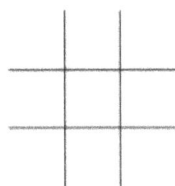 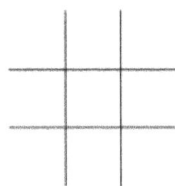

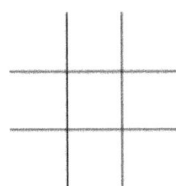 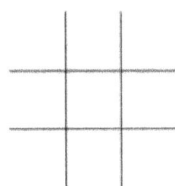 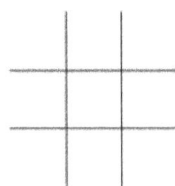

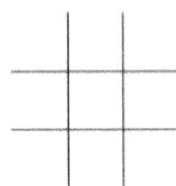 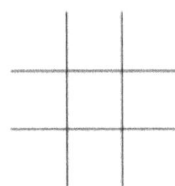 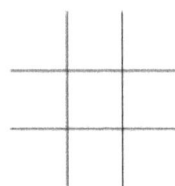

Mazes

Start at the entrance to the maze and then work your way through it, until to exit the other end...

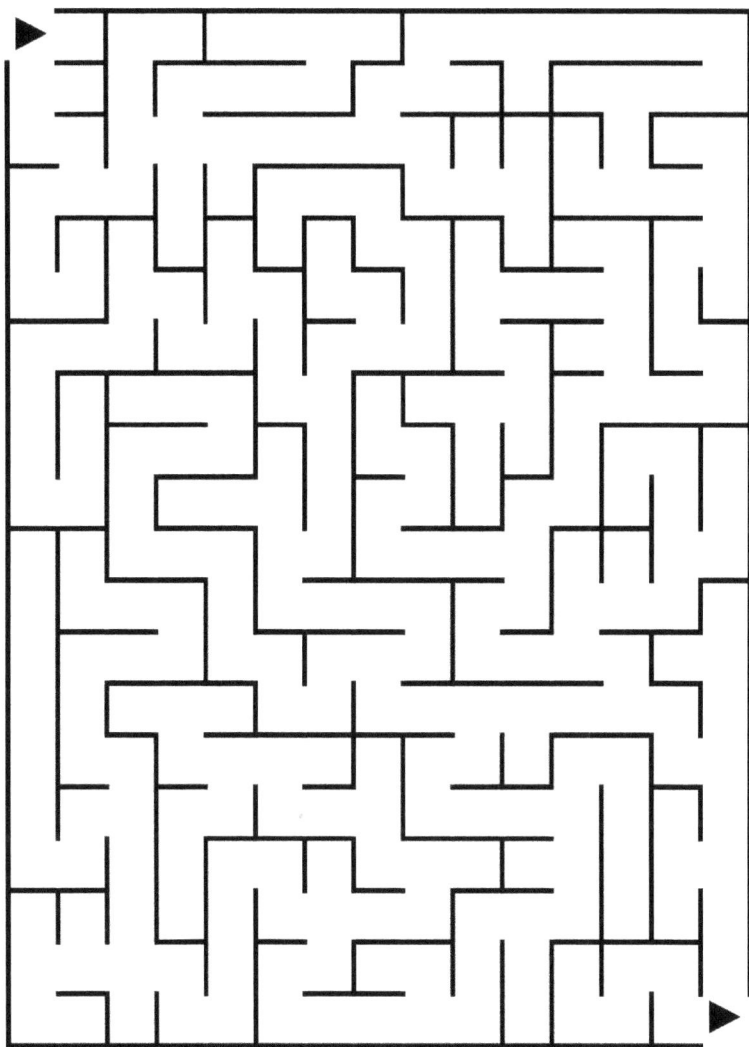

Word search instructions

In a word search puzzle, words are placed within a grid of random letters.

The words themselves are searched within the grid.

The words can go in any direction:

- left to right →

- right to left ←

- top to bottom ↓

- bottom to top ↑

- diagonal up or down ↗ ↘

Word search 1

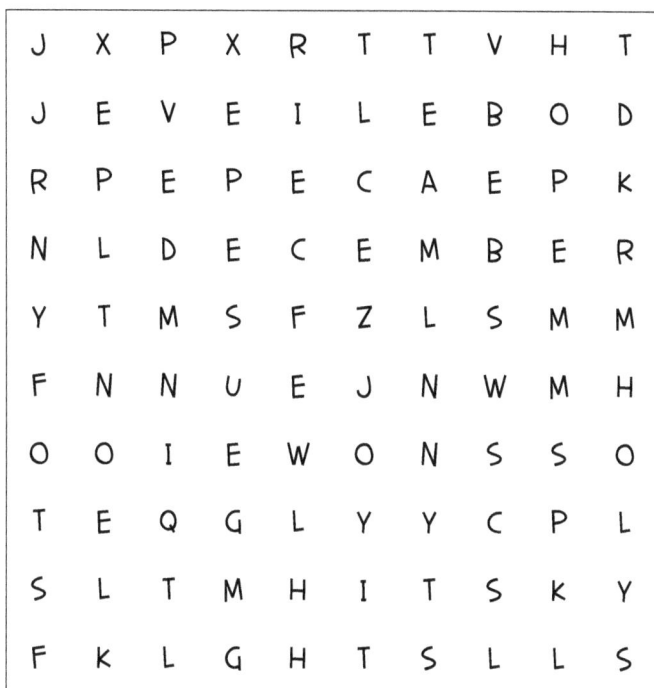

J	X	P	X	R	T	T	V	H	T
J	E	V	E	I	L	E	B	O	D
R	P	E	P	E	C	A	E	P	K
N	L	D	E	C	E	M	B	E	R
Y	T	M	S	F	Z	L	S	M	M
F	N	N	U	E	J	N	W	M	H
O	O	I	E	W	O	N	S	S	O
T	E	Q	G	L	Y	Y	C	P	L
S	L	T	M	H	I	T	S	K	Y
F	K	L	G	H	T	S	L	L	S

BELIEVE   JOY   SILENT
DECEMBER   NIGHT   SNOW
HOLY   NOEL
HOPE   PEACE

Word search 2

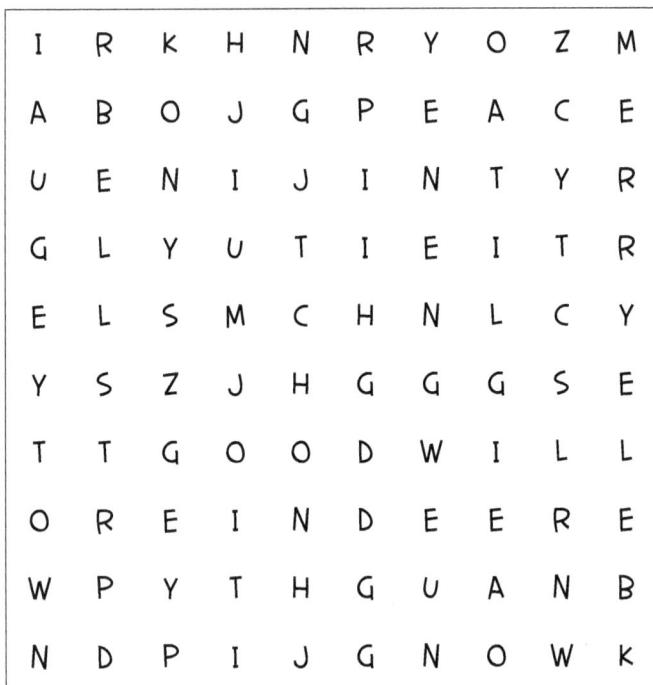

I	R	K	H	N	R	Y	O	Z	M
A	B	O	J	G	P	E	A	C	E
U	E	N	I	J	I	N	T	Y	R
G	L	Y	U	T	I	E	I	T	R
E	L	S	M	C	H	N	L	C	Y
Y	S	Z	J	H	G	G	G	S	E
T	T	G	O	O	D	W	I	L	L
O	R	E	I	N	D	E	E	R	E
W	P	Y	T	H	G	U	A	N	B
N	D	P	I	J	G	N	O	W	K

BELLS   MERRY   REINDEER
BRIGHT   NAUGHTY   SLEIGH
GOODWILL   NICE
JINGLE   PEACE

Word search 3

S	O	N	X	S	E	P	E	X	J
H	Y	J	E	S	U	S	T	A	R
E	W	S	Q	M	Z	G	Y	Y	Q
P	M	B	D	B	G	U	O	R	M
H	A	B	S	T	A	B	L	E	U
E	N	U	O	L	S	B	K	A	N
R	G	W	I	S	E	V	Y	A	M
D	E	S	O	G	Y	G	I	V	G
S	R	G	K	C	B	G	N	H	N
S	T	P	B	G	G	Q	N	A	G

ANGEL	MANGER	STAR
BABY	MEN	WISE
INN	SHEPHERDS	
JESUS	STABLE	

Word search 4

G	Z	L	W	W	P	V	G	F	P
S	G	P	B	Y	T	O	M	N	O
H	W	W	R	A	D	C	R	V	P
R	P	Z	F	E	U	N	B	T	C
E	N	A	C	X	S	B	A	R	O
E	E	R	T	R	T	E	L	C	R
E	R	R	I	B	B	O	N	E	N
D	G	V	Q	L	I	G	H	T	S
S	Y	M	L	E	S	N	I	T	S
L	W	R	A	P	P	I	N	G	L

BAUBLES   POPCORN   TREE
CANDY   PRESENTS   WRAPPING
CANE   RIBBON
LIGHTS   TINSEL

Word search 5

U	I	L	G	T	E	Z	M	N	R
S	E	Y	E	Q	S	L	K	A	F
P	T	C	C	S	M	B	C	X	H
R	A	U	U	Y	S	P	M	W	P
O	X	Q	N	A	Z	U	E	C	O
U	A	S	D	T	S	I	R	A	U
T	J	O	F	N	S	D	R	B	V
S	E	T	U	R	K	E	Y	R	N
P	U	D	D	I	N	G	H	W	Q
Y	R	R	E	B	N	A	R	C	I

BRUSSEL   MERRY   TURKEY
CHESTNUTS   PUDDING
CRANBERRY   SAUCE
HAM   SPROUTS

119

Word search 6

W	A	R	M	L	A	C	V	L	D
O	R	A	N	G	E	D	R	I	Y
Y	O	J	N	E	N	Y	O	J	G
L	U	F	H	T	I	A	F	R	R
C	H	E	R	U	B	L	A	Z	E
P	C	H	I	L	L	H	T	L	E
O	P	L	I	T	T	L	E	W	N
L	L	L	A	C	I	G	A	M	J
A	U	B	N	R	O	B	W	E	N
R	M	K	F	E	S	T	I	V	E

ADORE   FESTIVE   PLUM
CALM   GREEN   POLAR
CHERUB   MAGICAL
FAITHFUL   NEWBORN

Word search 7

U	K	K	U	K	U	V	Y	C	U
V	I	Q	E	V	I	T	S	E	F
U	T	S	Y	Y	F	N	H	D	P
Z	B	Y	I	A	T	Y	D	N	E
B	H	U	R	N	C	S	Z	X	A
G	X	R	R	G	G	I	O	U	C
C	M	G	U	E	N	I	X	R	E
T	H	G	I	L	H	U	N	D	F
O	R	A	H	E	X	C	H	G	U
K	R	E	M	M	I	H	S	L	L

ANGEL   HUNGRY   SHIMMER
CHERUB   KIND   SINGING
FESTIVE   LIGHT
FROSTY   PEACEFUL

Sudoku Instructions

The smaller sudoku puzzle grid consists of 6 rows, 6 columns, and 6 inner boxes.

A completed puzzle has the numbers 1-6 in each row, in each column, and in each inner box.

To start, some numbers are removed.

Solving the puzzle means figuring out what the numbers to fill back in. By looking at each row, column and inner box, work out the missing numbers and fill them in.

For example, in the puzzle below:

➢ the number 6 is all the columns except the 5th, and all the rows except the 6th.

➢ in the first box, the numbers 2 and 5 are missing in the first column. Looking at the 2nd column, we have a 5, so then that must go in the 1st column, as you can't have repeat numbers.

		6		3	
4	2	3		5	6
2			6	4	5
6	4		3	1	2
3	6		5		
	5				

5	1	6	2	3	4
4	2	3	1	5	6
2	3	1	6	4	5
6	4	5	3	1	2
3	6	4	5	2	1
1	5	2	4	6	3

Sudoku 6 x6 Puzzle 1

6		5		4	
				5	
	3		4		
	4	1	3		5
	5	4	2		6
		2	5		

1 2 3 4 5 6

Sudoku 6 x6 Puzzle 2

		4	1		
5					
3	5	2			
	1	6	3	5	
		3	5		4
2			6		3

1 2 3 4 5 6

Sudoku 6 x6 Puzzle 3

2	4	6	5		
5	3			2	6
6	1	3			4
4		2		6	
3		4			5
		5			2

1 2 3 4 5 6

Sudoku 6 x6 Puzzle 4

4				2	
3		1	6	4	
	3		5	6	
		6	4		
5	4	2			6
		3		5	

1 2 3 4 5 6

Sudoku 6 x6 Puzzle 5

6			2	4	1
2		4	5		
		6		5	
	4		6	1	
	6		1	3	5
		1			6

1 2 3 4 5 6

Solutions

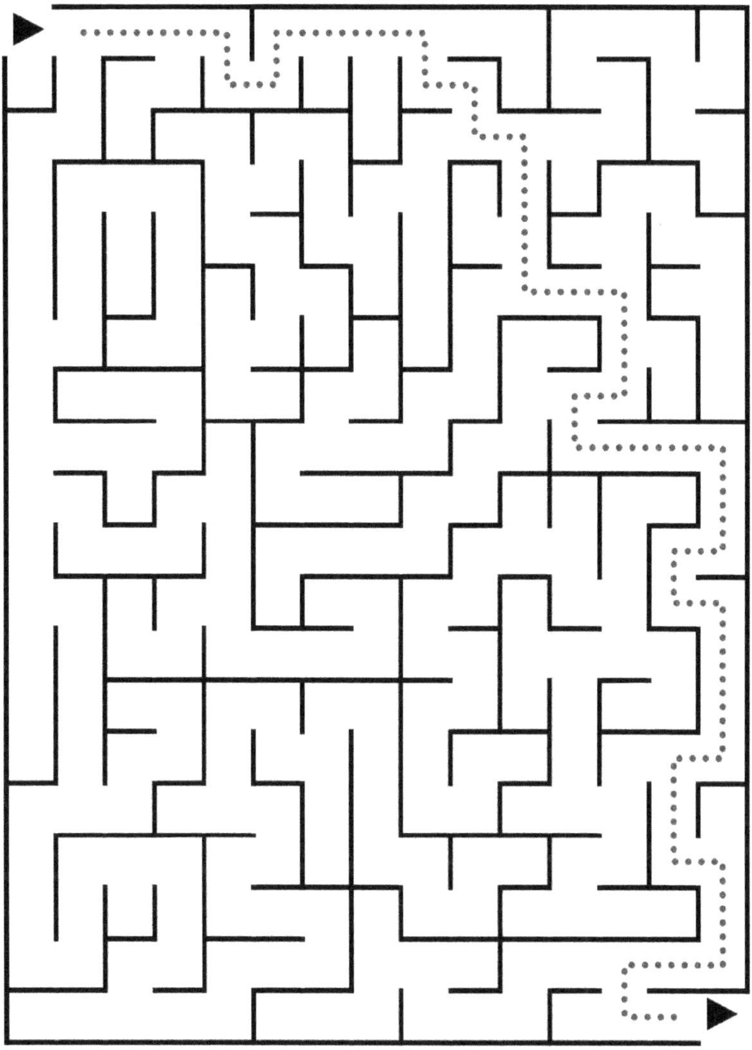

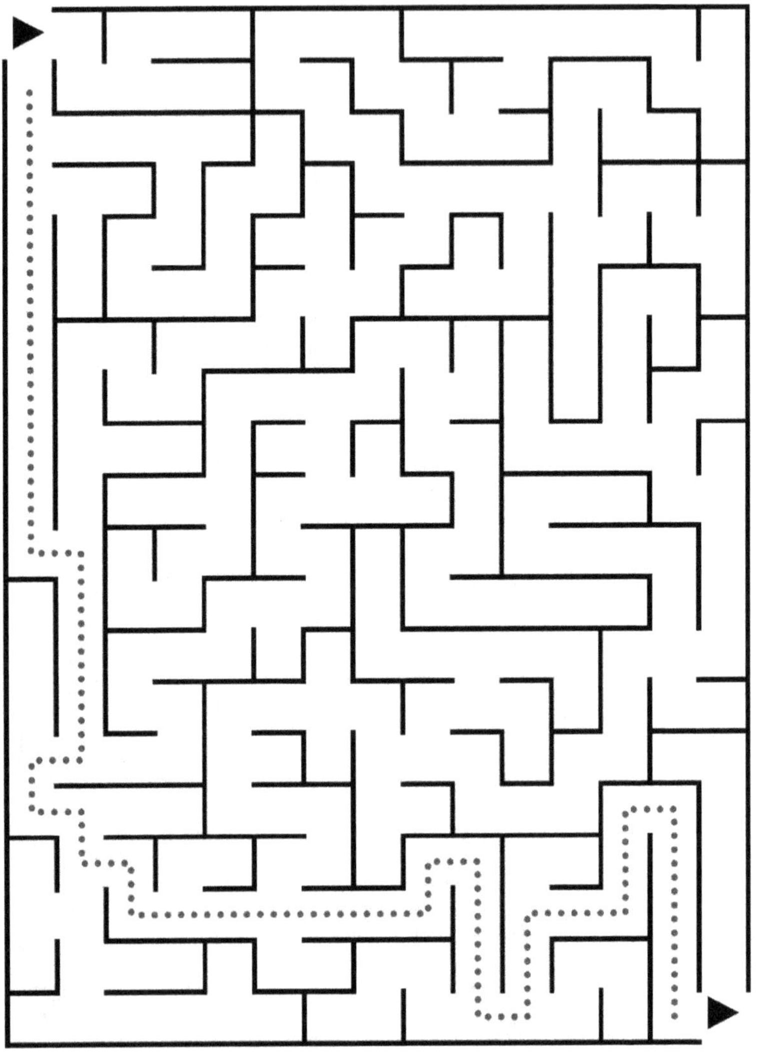

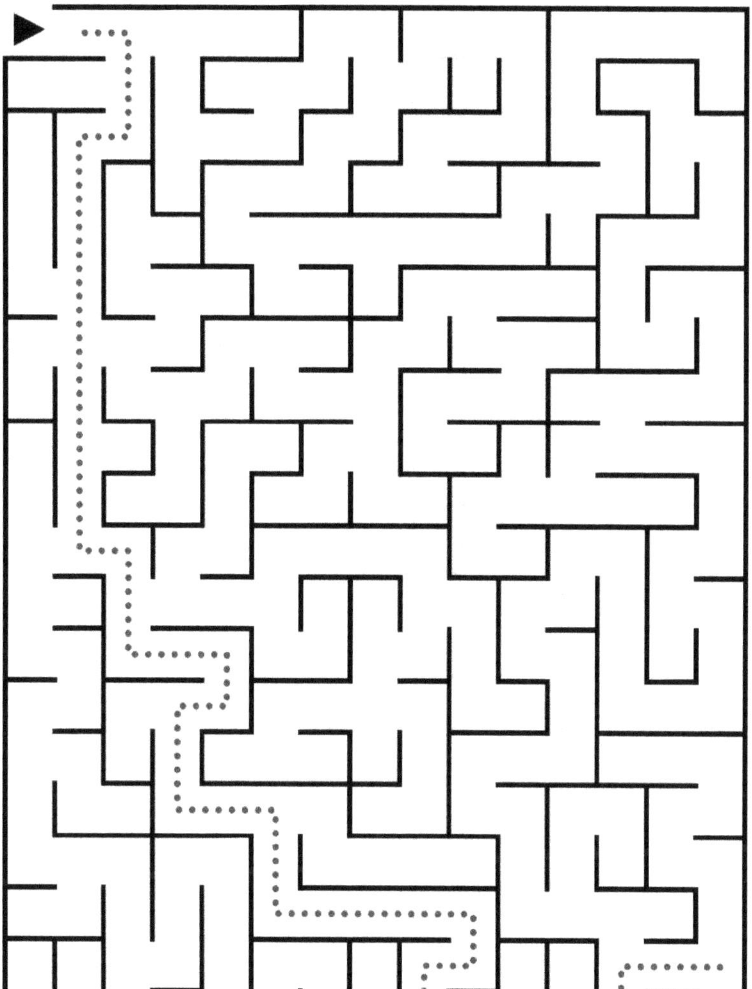

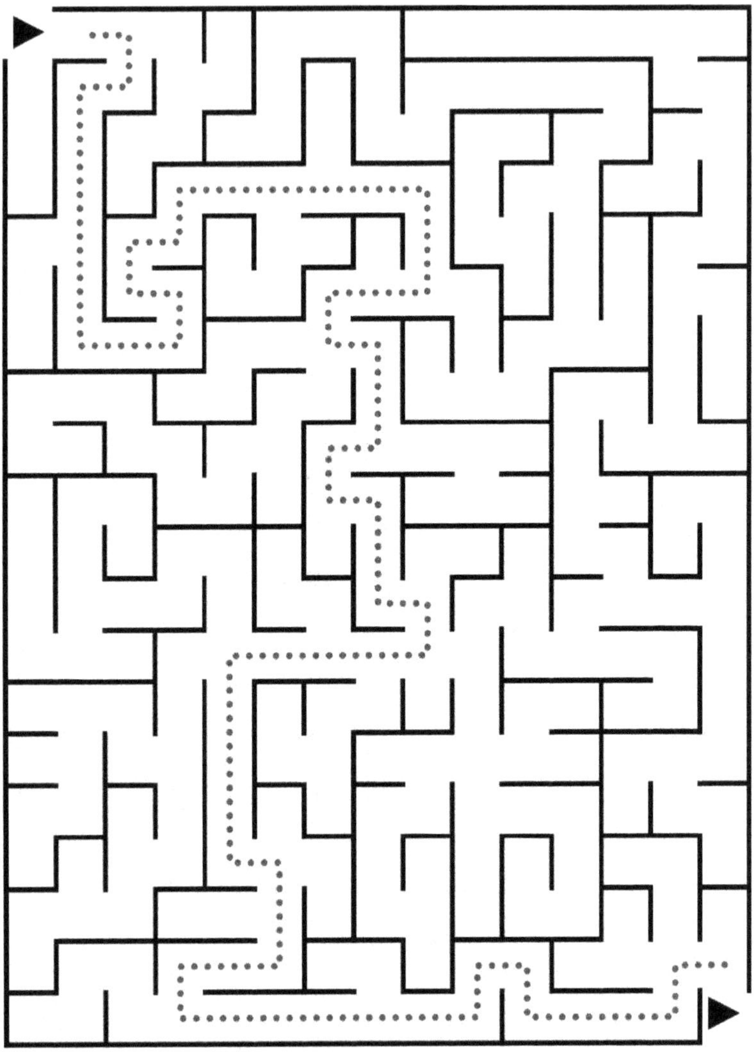

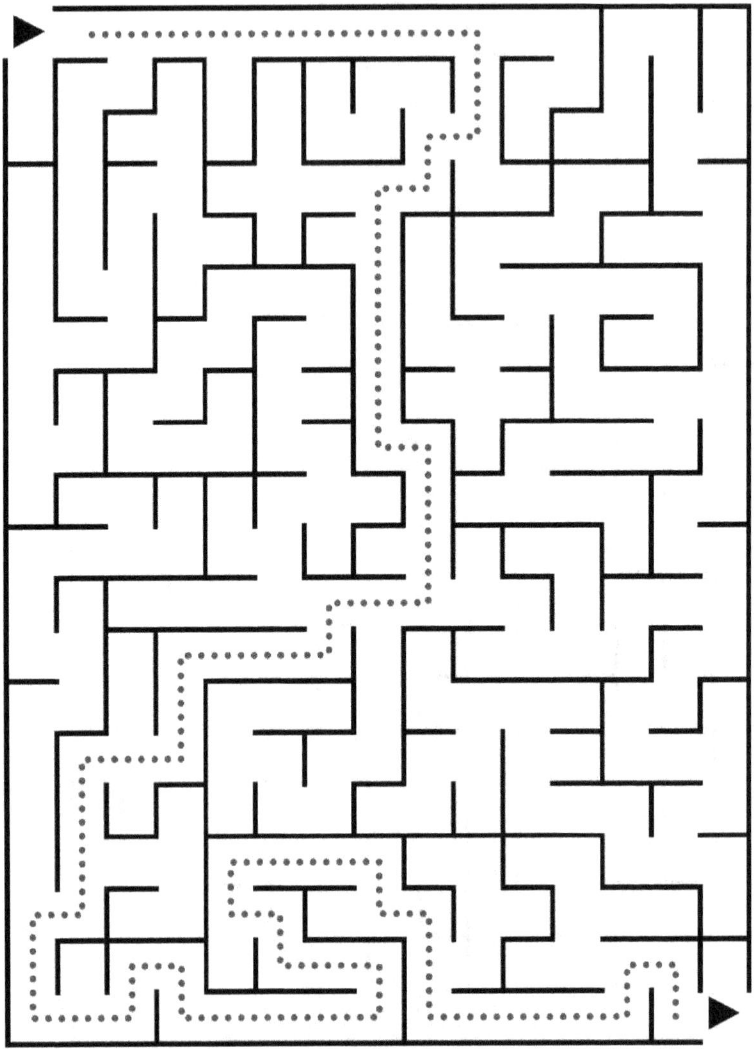

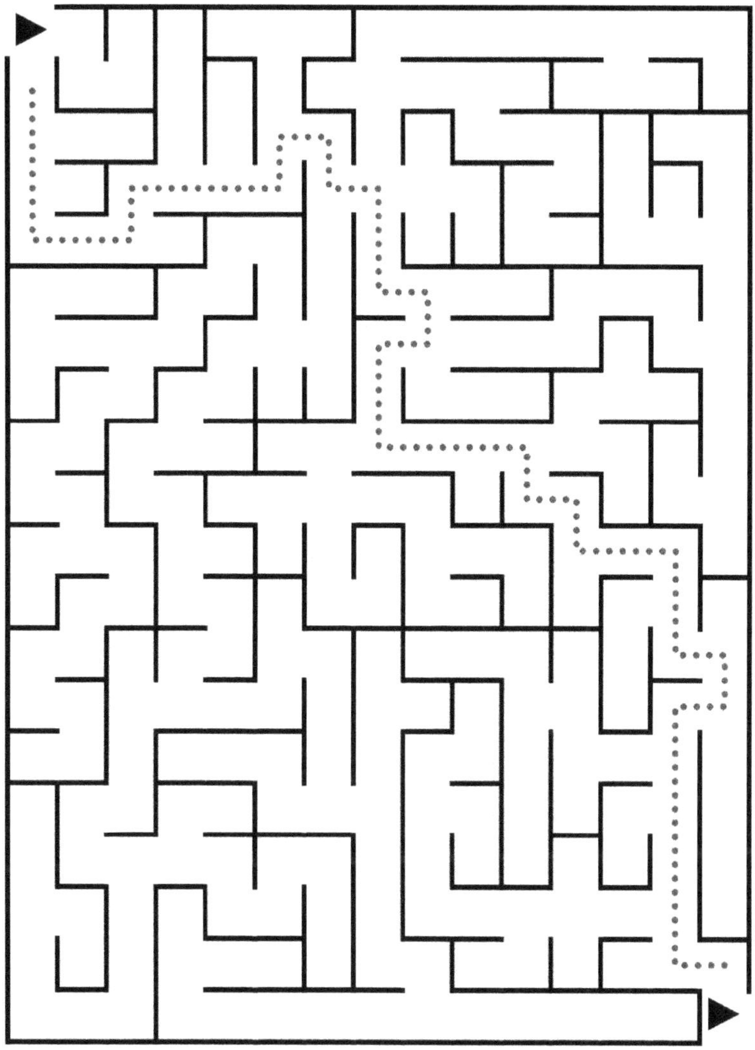

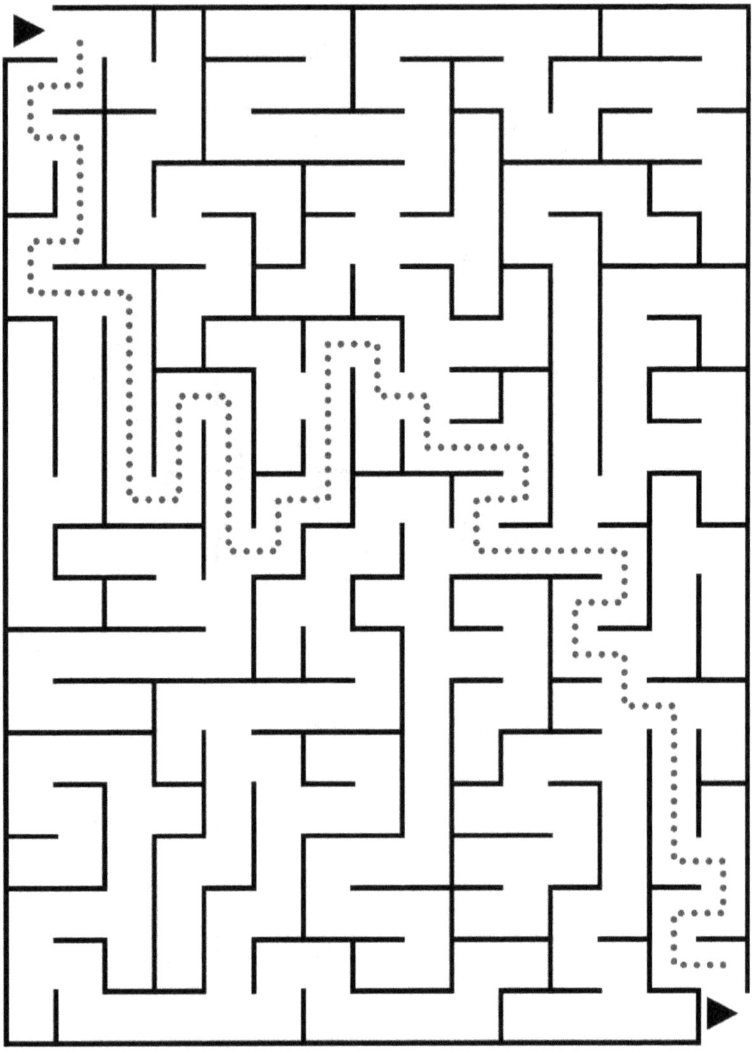

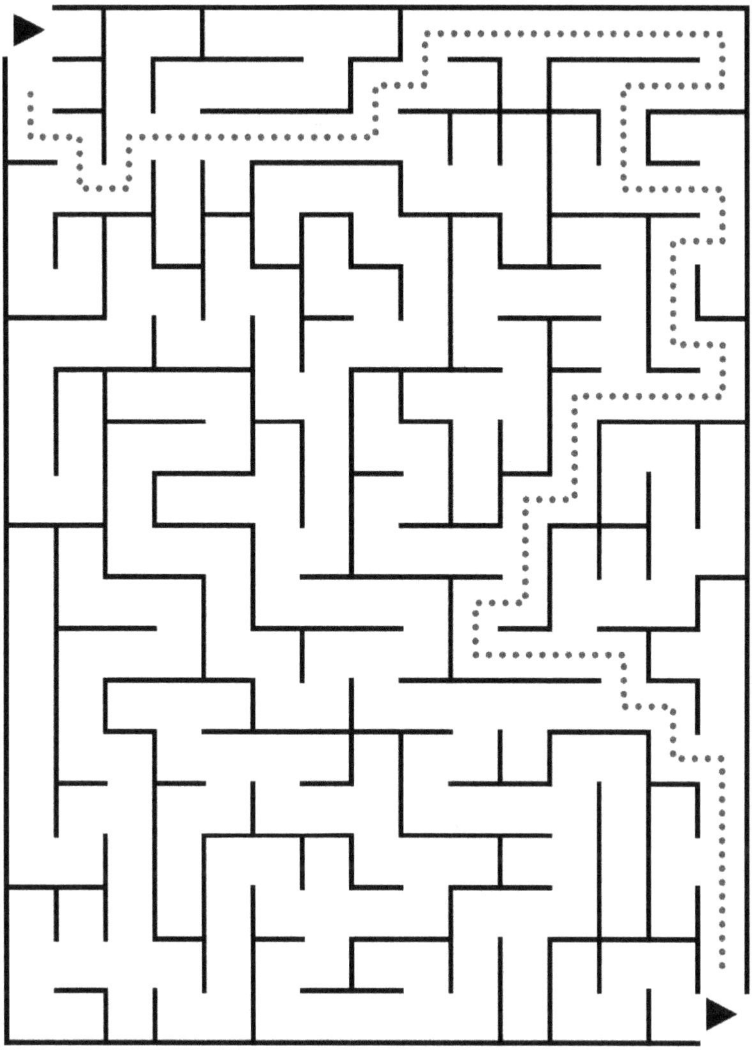

Word search 1

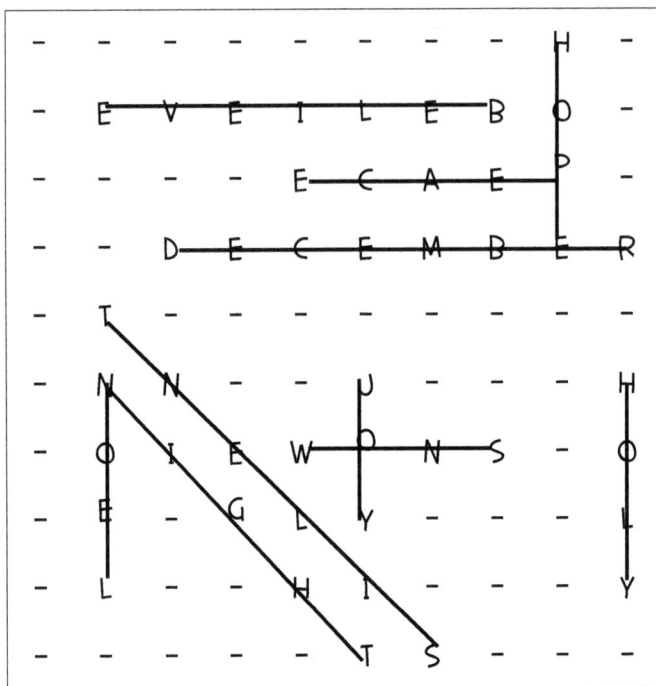

Word search 2

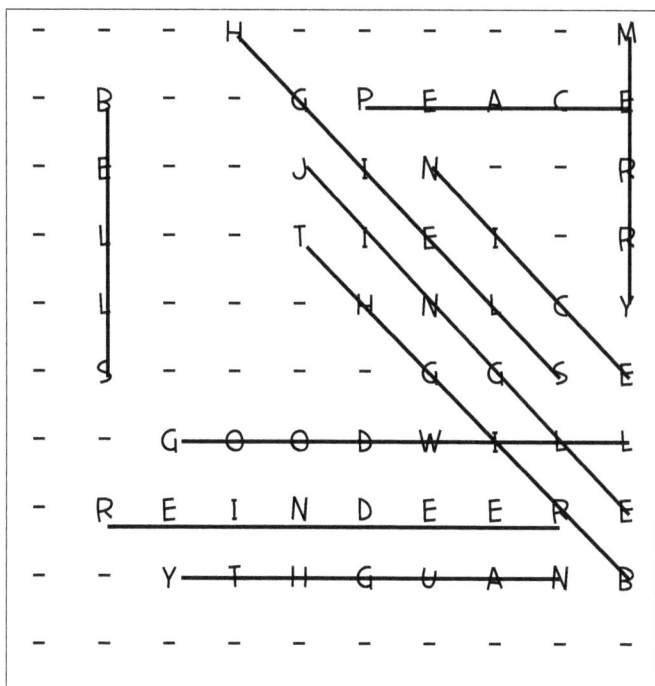

141

Word search 3

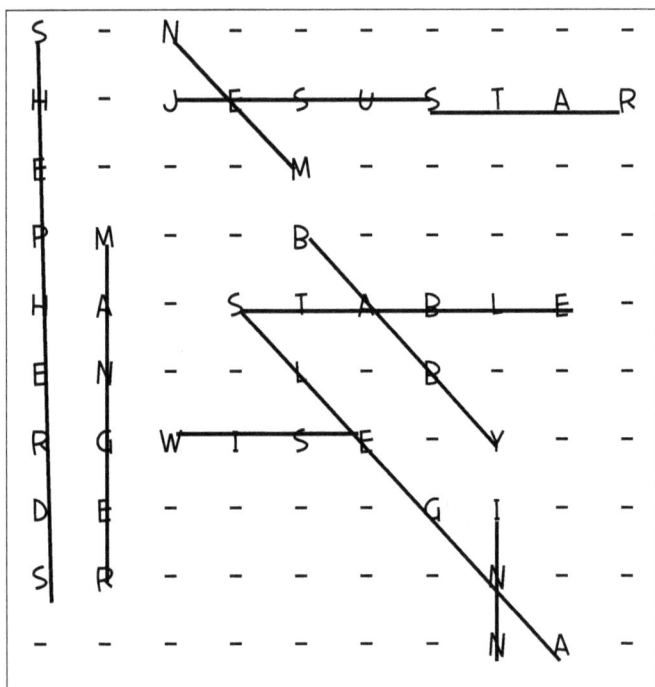

```
S   -   N   -   -   -   -   -   -   -
H   -   J   E   S   U   S   T   A   R
E   -   -   -   M   -   -   -   -   -
P   M   -   -   B   -   -   -   -   -
H   A   -   S   T   A   B   L   E   -
E   N   -   -   L   -   B   -   -   -
R   G   W   I   S   E   -   Y   -   -
D   E   -   -   -   -   G   I   -   -
S   R   -   -   -   -   N   -   -
-   -   -   -   -   -   -   N   A   -
```

Word search 4

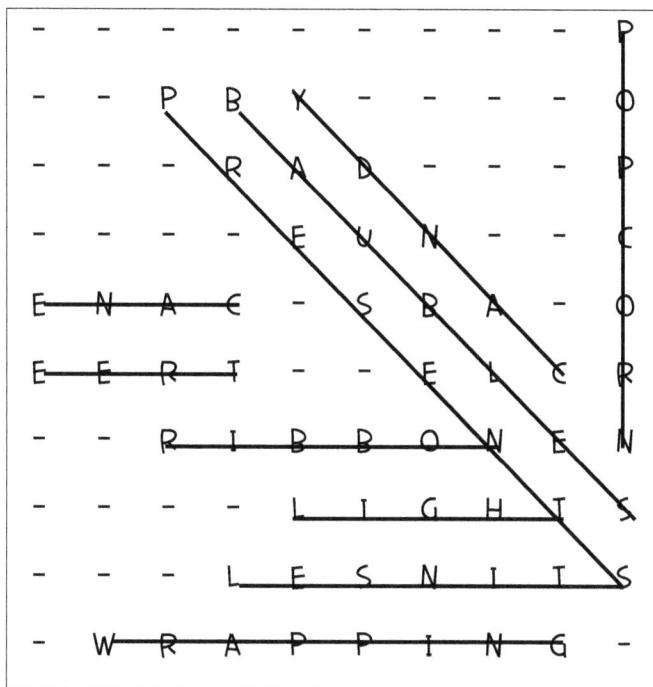

```
-  -  -  -  -  -  -  -  -  P
-  -  P  B  X  -  -  -  -  O
-  -  -  R  A  D  -  -  -  P
-  -  -  E  U  N  -  -  -  C
E  N  A  C  -  S  B  A  -  O
E  E  R  T  -  -  E  L  C  R
-  -  R  I  B  B  O  N  E  N
-  -  -  -  L  I  G  H  T  S
-  -  -  L  E  S  N  I  T  S
-  W  R  A  P  P  I  N  G  -
```

Word search 5

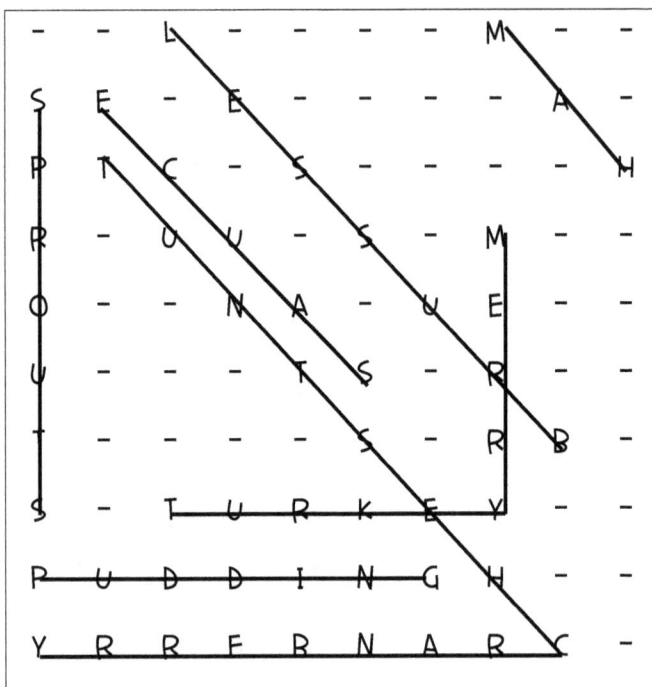

```
-  -  L  -  -  -  -  M  -  -
S  E  -  E  -  -  -  -  A  -
P  T  C  -  S  -  -  -  -  H
R  -  U  U  -  S  -  M  -  -
O  -  -  N  A  -  U  E  -  -
U  -  -  -  T  S  -  R  -  -
T  -  -  -  -  S  -  R  B  -
S  -  T  U  R  K  E  Y  -  -
P  U  D  D  I  N  G  H  -  -
Y  R  R  E  B  N  A  R  C  -
```

Word search 6

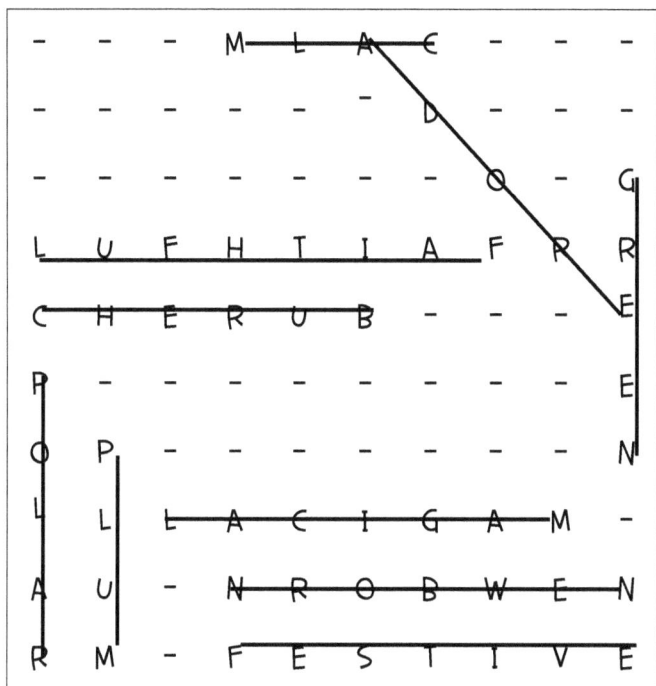

- - - M L A E - - -
- - - - - - D - - -
- - - - - - O - G
L U F H T I A F R R
C H E R U B - - - E
P - - - - - - - E
O P - - - - - - - N
- L L A C I G A M -
A U - N R O B W E N
R M - F E S T I V E

Word search 7

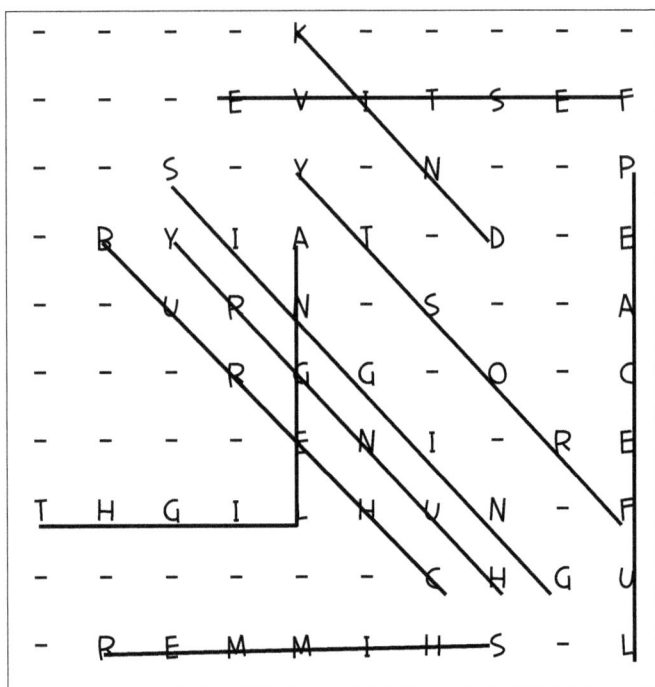

```
-   -   -   -   K   -   -   -   -   -
-   -   -   E   V   I   T   S   E   F
-   -   S   -   Y   -   N   -   -   P
-   R   Y   I   A   T   -   D   -   E
-   -   U   R   N   -   S   -   -   A
-   -   -   R   G   G   -   O   -   C
-   -   -   -   E   N   I   -   R   E
T   H   G   I   L   H   U   N   -   F
-   -   -   -   -   -   C   H   G   U
-   R   E   M   M   I   H   S   -   L
```

Puzzle #1

6	2	5	1	4	3
4	1	3	6	5	2
5	3	6	4	2	1
2	4	1	3	6	5
3	5	4	2	1	6
1	6	2	5	3	4

Puzzle #2

6	2	4	1	3	5
5	3	1	2	4	6
3	5	2	4	6	1
4	1	6	3	5	2
1	6	3	5	2	4
2	4	5	6	1	3

Puzzle #3

2	4	6	5	3	1
5	3	1	4	2	6
6	1	3	2	5	4
4	5	2	1	6	3
3	2	4	6	1	5
1	6	5	3	4	2

Puzzle #4

4	6	5	1	2	3
3	2	1	6	4	5
2	3	4	5	6	1
1	5	6	4	3	2
5	4	2	3	1	6
6	1	3	2	5	4

Puzzle #5

6	5	3	2	4	1
2	1	4	5	6	3
1	2	6	3	5	4
3	4	5	6	1	2
4	6	2	1	3	5
5	3	1	4	2	6

About the author

Deirdre Shahzad spent 15 years working in the travel industry and has 3 children, 2 of which have special needs.

She is based in Ireland where she hopes to help and encourage parents of special needs to travel and take holidays with their children.

Her website is:

www.autismandadventures.com.